Draw Close

Draw Close

A CREATIVE COMPANION FOR LENT

STEPHANIE B. DUNN

UPPER ROOM BOOKS®
NASHVILLE

Cover design: McKenzie Baker
Cover imagery: Stephanie B. Dunn
Interior design and typesetting: PerfecType | Nashville, TN

ISBN: 978-0-8358-2058-5

Printed in the United States of America.

Contents

CONTENTS

CONTENTS

An Invitation to Get Creative

To start, let's get something out of the way: I am not a professional artist. I started doodling with a pack of watercolor markers and eventually learned how to use those markers for creating small watercolor pieces. I had been using my markers for a while when I noticed that my practice had become a form of prayer. For Lent, I decided to put together a list of texts and prompts for myself and shared it with others as a way of creating a community of prayer through creative practices. Participants used media of all kinds. A musician composed hymns inspired by the readings; a photographer shared images that helped connect with a psalm; friends shared their daily sketches. What you have in your hands is an extension of a growing community of prayer, people who are growing in their faith by engaging their creativity—not as professionals but as people created by a God who invites us to co-create in a world that desperately needs wonder and imagination.

In these pages, you will find an invitation. This invitation comes with a sense of curiosity about where the journey will take you and a promise that you will be surprised by what you discover. As there is with all spiritual disciplines, the invitation is to grow closer to God and others. The growth here will take you on your own unique path. The invitation is for you to engage your creativity, looking to the scriptures with an open playfulness. Your response is just that. It's *yours*.

The structure of *Draw Close* is simple. For each day of the season of Lent, you are invited to approach the biblical text with playful creativity. Each day's entry has a simple format. On one page, you will find a biblical text, a word with a brief definition, how that word is used in the text or in tradition, and a prayer. The second page is blank space. This open space is for you. In this space, you are invited to respond using whatever creative medium you choose. It could be sketching, painting, poetry, or composition: whatever you already have, already use, or have always wanted to try.

Creativity is about process. So is spiritual practice. Spiritual disciplines are not about what is produced. In the same way that there is no "right" way to pray, there is no "right" way to do *Draw Close*. Don't worry about the end result—your creative responses do not need to be "Instagram worthy." Focus on the process of creation and what you discover about yourself and God along the way. Focus on what you experience through the readings and the journey of the season.

Creativity as a spiritual discipline offers us a spaciousness that in many ways is countercultural. Spiritual disciplines can be seen as an act of resistance to our Western world's demand to produce on rigid timelines. As you pick up *Draw Close*, open yourself to the rhythm of creativity. You might miss some days here and there. That is okay. Just move at the pace of the creative human that you are.

The scriptures we traditionally explore during Lent are filled with anticipation and curiosity. The stories and the poetry of the Psalms lend themselves to a creative response. The scriptures that tell of Jesus' journey to the cross invite us to open our hearts and pay attention to God's work in both the challenges and the beauty of the world in and around us.

This Lent, I invite you to open yourself to what is possible.

Grab your pencils, piano, or paint! Let's draw close and see what God is up to!

A Note on Sundays in Lent:
An Invitation to Notice

On Sundays in *Draw Close*, you will notice there is a pause. This isn't intended to be a time to "turn off" your creative practices; rather, it is an invitation to "tune in." When I started dabbling in watercolors, I noticed that I paid attention to the world differently. My eyes were more tuned into the nuances in the world around me. Trees weren't just "green"; they were a lovely contrast between sap green with pops of green-gold and millions of other tiny, beautiful shades. I began to pay attention to what I paid attention to. I have always felt a deep connection to God in the natural world, but my creative practices helped me to notice more of the beautifully brilliant world around me and served as a powerful invitation to pause and experience the world more deeply.

On Sundays in *Draw Close*, you will find an invitation to push pause, to tune in, to pay attention to what you are paying attention to. The format for Sundays is different from the rest of the days of the week, offering space to pause, breathe deeply, and reflect. In this pause, may you discover God's beautifully brilliant work in the world around you.

An Outline for Small-Group Use of *Draw Close*

Creative practices have an inherently expansive quality. When we share our creativity with one another, our imperfect work invites others to engage their own creativity. Because creativity nurtures sharing communities, *Draw Close* lends itself to use within a small group. The outline below is a suggestion for small groups working through *Draw Close*. Feel free to adapt or move in whichever direction serves your small group best. One person may act as a group's leader every week, or group members may rotate roles.

Opening

God is our refuge and strength
A help always near in times of great trouble.
That's why we won't be afraid when the world falls apart. (Ps 46:1-2a)

Opening Prayer

Creative and creating God, how wonderful are the works of your hands.
You breathed life into us, inviting us to participate in your acts of love and mercy.
In a season of repentance and wondering, we return to you, opening our hands, lifting up our voices,
    pursuing you on our journey.
In your presence, O God, we come near.
Open our hearts to see your creative work in one another and in your world. Amen.

Scripture

Choose a scripture to read from the week in *Draw Close*.

Sharing

- What scripture passage from this week did you connect with creatively?
- How did you grow in your understanding of scripture through your creative practices this week?
- What did you create that you would like to share with the group?
- What scripture passage was challenging to your faith? To your creative practice?

Praying Together

Invite group members to share people and situations that they would like to hold together in prayer.

God, you are mystery and wonder.
We stand in awe of your work in and among us.
Come near to the people and places that we're holding close;
Come near to those whom we haven't named;
Come near to those who are forgotten.
Give us the gift of imagination to see a world where pain and suffering are no more,
that we might walk on your path of peace-making and justice.
Amen.

Departing

As we walk through the Lenten journey,
may our creative God work in you,
giving you visions of peace, justice, and reconciliation
that you might participate in God's work in the world.
Amen.

Ash Wednesday

Isaiah 58:1–12

> **ash**
>
> (ash) *noun*:
>
> ———————————
>
> fine gray particles that remain once a substance has burned completely down

Then you will call, and the Lord will answer;
    you will cry for help, and God will say, "I'm here".
                                            —Isaiah 58:9

Ashes have been used throughout the church's history as a symbol for repentance and mortality. Ash Wednesday marks the beginning of Lent, the forty-day preparation period (not including Sundays) for Easter. On Ash Wednesday, churches around the world place ashes in the shape of a cross on worshipers' foreheads. As the pastor places the ashes, they may say, "From dust you came, and to dust you shall return," or "Repent, and believe the gospel."

As you think about ashes, wonder about how repentance and mortality will show up for you this Lent. How will you turn to God? How will you remember that your life is not your own, but is made full in Jesus Christ?

We call out to you, O God, and say, "Here we are." Remind us of your presence throughout this Lenten journey that we may faithfully follow you. Amen.

Psalm 91:2, 9-16

> **refuge**
>
> ('re-(ˌ)fyüj) *noun*:
> _____
>
> a place that offers protection or shelter
> when someone is in danger

Whenever you cry out to me, I'll answer.
I'll be with you in troubling times.
I'll save you and glorify you.

—Psalm 91:15

Throughout scripture, the word "refuge" is used to describe God's protection for those who return to God when there is uncertainty or danger.

In the season of Lent, our own brokenness and the brokenness of the world are laid before God. We lay our sins before God, knowing that, in our humanity, we often miss the mark in our love for God and neighbor. We also lay before God the sins of the world. The world is not as it should be. Lent is a time for bringing all this brokenness to God. We remember that when we repent of, or "turn away, from," our sins, God offers forgiveness and a refuge, a place of protection and shelter in an uncertain world.

From what do you need refuge? Where is God offering refuge to you?

You, O God, are our refuge and our fortress. Your love is a safe place in a
world of danger and fear. Help us to draw near to you. Amen.

Psalm 32

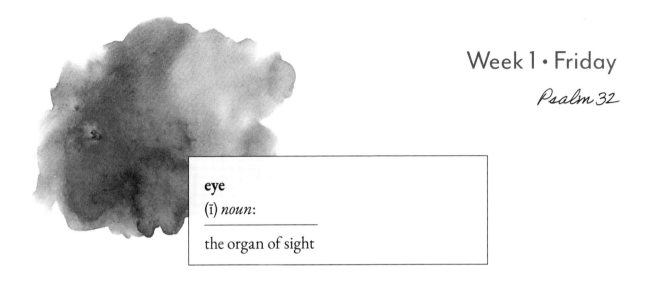

> **eye**
> (ī) *noun*:
> _____
> the organ of sight

I will instruct you and teach you
    about the direction you should go.
I'll advise you and keep my eye on you.
                                —Psalm 32:8

Psalm 32 is a song of celebration for the forgiveness and restoration that God pours out when we bring all of ourselves, the beautiful and the broken, before the Lord. The psalmist uses the eye to describe God's caring watchfulness.

Lent is a heavy season. There is a lot of emphasis on sin and brokenness. It's easy to fall into despair, wondering what good there could possibly be in the world and in us. Psalm 32 reminds us that joy and God's forgiveness are always on the other side of confession. In a broken world, God is faithfully watching over us. On the other side of our despair, there is joy to be found!

How is God's watchful eye caring for you?

There are no secrets from you, O Lord. Your watchful eye is always looking to care
for us. Help us to look to you for your guidance and protection. Amen.

gift

(gift) *noun*:
_____

something given without anything due or
expected in return

But the free gift of Christ isn't like Adam's failure. If many people died through
what one person did wrong, God's grace is multiplied even more for many
people with the gift—of the one person Jesus Christ—that comes through
grace.

—Romans 5:15

Grace is at the heart of the gospel; the good news of what God has done and is doing through Jesus
Christ. God's gift to the world is grace. Grace is the understanding that God's love is freely and
fully poured out on the world and all that is in it. That's a very big gift!

Lent is a season of paradox, a time for remembering that many things are true at the same time. In
these verses from Romans, the apostle Paul digs into the paradox of sin and grace. We experience the
brokenness of the world every day. Yet it is also true that God's love is at work in us and in the world
around us. This work of love in a broken world is the gift of grace.

How do you experience God's gift of grace?

*We live in a broken world, O God. Even in pain and despair, your love is at work. Thank
you, God, for your grace. Help us to carry your grace and love into the world. Amen.*

FIRST SUNDAY

in Lent

Today is Sunday. Push pause. Tune in.

Pay attention to what you're paying attention to today.

What do you notice?

What do you see?
What do you smell?
What do you hear?
What do you taste?
What do you feel?

Use the following page to capture or respond to what you are noticing.

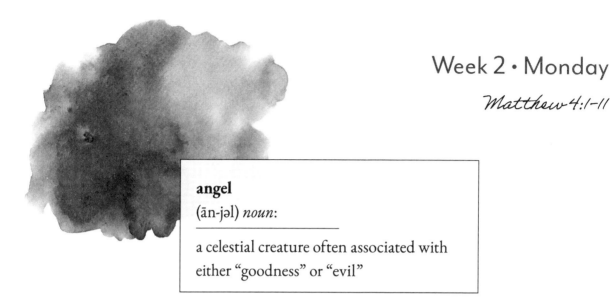

angel

(ān-jəl) *noun*:

a celestial creature often associated with either "goodness" or "evil"

Jesus responded, "Go away, Satan, because it's written, *You will worship the Lord your God and serve only him.*" The devil left him, and angels came and took care of him.

—Matthew 4:10-11

Throughout scripture, angels are understood to be intermediaries between God and people. In the Gospels, angels are often present in some of the most defining moments of Jesus' life. In the story of the temptation of Jesus, angels show up to care for Jesus after the devil has tempted him for forty days in the wilderness. In Jesus' faithfulness, God offers protection and care.

Lent is a time to acknowledge those things that take our attention away from God. The practice of giving something up for Lent brings us closer to God by enabling us to focus our attention on God—not on other things that often distract us. The story of Jesus' temptation reminds us that there are always things that draw us away from God. In this story, we see God's compassionate care is present when we need it most.

How have you experienced God's compassion and care?

We come to you, O God, knowing that you are always extending your compassion and care. Help us to look to you in all things, making you the center of our lives, so that we may extend your compassion and care to others. Amen.

> **mountain**
>
> (ˈmau̇n-tᵊn) *noun*:
> _____
>
> a large mound of earth that is larger than
> a steep hill

> I raise my eyes toward the mountains.
> > Where will my help come from?
> My help comes from the LORD,
> > the maker of heaven and earth.
>
> —Psalm 121:1-2

In scripture, the word "mountain" calls us to pay special attention. In biblical tradition, wherever there are mountains, God is showing up. The psalmist begins Psalm 121 by looking to the mountains, knowing he will certainly find God's presence and help there.

Our Christian faith holds space for us to acknowledge that many things can be true. Our world is overwhelmed with conflict and violence. And yet, we know that peace and justice are possible. The psalmist reminds us to look to God for help and protection in all things. With God as our guide, we can move forward, knowing that God is with us.

Where are you looking for God to show up around you? How can you practice confidence in God's protection?

Mighty God, you are always with us. Help us to look to you as
our guide and protector in all our lives. Amen.

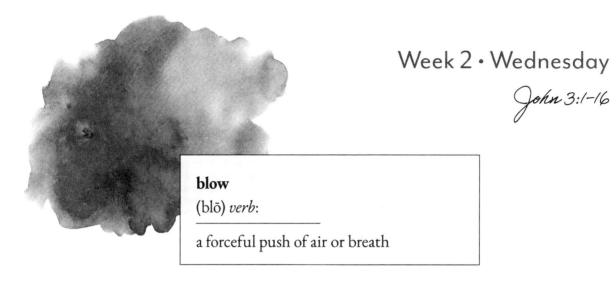

John 3:1–16

blow

(blō) *verb*:

———————————

a forceful push of air or breath

God's Spirit blows wherever it wishes. You hear its sound, but you don't know where it comes from or where it is going. It's the same with everyone who is born of the Spirit.

—John 3:8

Just as wind and breath can be a bit mysterious, God is also mysterious. We experience God's mystery acutely in the Spirit. Our Christian understanding of the Spirit is as the life force that connects us to God. The Spirit is not bound by time or space. Jesus talks about the interconnectedness of a person's spirit to God's Spirit.

There is a mysteriousness to the season of Lent. While we know that ultimately we are headed toward the death of Good Friday and the resurrection of Easter, we cannot know what lies on the path that will get us there. Over and over again, Jesus reminds us that we are not alone in our uncertainty. The Spirit is always moving within and around us. It's a mystery, but we can be confident that God is with us.

How do you sense the Spirit at work within and around you on your Lenten journey?

Too often, we don't know where we're going or how we're going to get there, O God.
But with the promise of your presence, we step forward in faith knowing that your Spirit
is always at work within and around us. Thank you, God, for your presence. Amen.

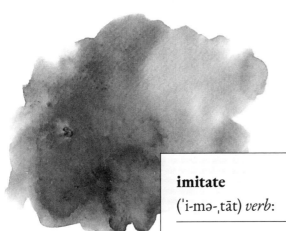

> **imitate**
>
> (ˈi-mə-ˌtāt) *verb*:
> _____
>
> to follow one's example, to mirror

Brothers and sisters, become imitators of me and watch those who live this way—you can use us as models.

—Philippians 3:17

In Paul's letter to Philippi, he wrote to encourage a community that was at risk of falling into old patterns that elevated personal gain over Christ-like service. Paul reminded the Philippians that they weren't alone in their pursuit to live like Christ. The community had Paul and other leaders whose lives they could imitate. They had one another, the beloved community, to provide support as they lived out Christ's love in the world.

It is easy to grow weary in our pursuit to live as followers of Jesus Christ. Throughout Lent, we pay special attention to growing in our capacity to follow Christ. This is no easy task. When left on our own, we will most certainly lose our way. As John Wesley noted in his journal, "The Bible knows nothing of solitary religion." We must look to one another in Christian community to grow in our likeness of Christ.

Who is a person in your life who imitates Christ well? How do you experience that person's faithfulness? How would you like to model your faith after that person's faith?

Thank you, God, for the people in our lives who show us what it is to be a follower of Jesus Christ. As we grow in your love, help us to imitate your love as well. Amen.

stand

(stánd) *verb*:

_____

to be upright on one's feet

Therefore, my brothers and sisters whom I love and miss, who are my joy and crown, stand firm in the Lord.

—Philippians 4:1

Paul observed those in the community of Philippi who were committed to faithfully following the crucified and resurrected Christ. From his own experience, he knew that the journey of discipleship was filled with sacrifice and persecution. He wrote to this community with gratitude for their faithfulness and encouraged them to carry on with confidence, standing firm in the Lord.

By God's grace, we do not travel the Lenten road alone. The humble path of discipleship is never easy. Just as Paul reminded the Philippians, we are reminded that we are surrounded by others who help us to be courageous as we move forward in faith. Be encouraged, dear one. God is with you; you are not alone. Stand firm in the Lord!

How have you been encouraged to stand firm in the Lord? Who could you encourage in their faith journey?

God, it is easy to grow weary as we walk in your way. We give thanks that we do not walk this journey alone. Help us to look to you and one another as we stand firm in your way of life and love. Amen.

touch

('təch) *verb*:

_____

to come physically close to the point of contact

But Jesus came and touched them. "Get up," he said. "Don't be afraid."

—Matthew 17:7

This story is full of dramatic imagery. God is surely present here on a very high mountain with an overshadowing cloud and dazzling clothes. There's even a voice, repeating the words from Jesus' baptism, "This is my Son." This time, the voice instructs those gathered to "listen to him!" This story demands attention. It's important to stay tuned in, even after the lights have been turned down and the heavenly voice has gone silent. It's in the seemingly mundane act that Jesus invites us to a fuller understanding of who he is.

Haptomai is the Greek word translated here as *to touch*. This word is often used in Jesus' miracles, where he came physically close to those on the margins. In their chaos, he came near enough to touch them, offering healing and wholeness.

How do you sense God's healing touch in a chaotic world?

*God, even when chaos swirls around us, you are with us. Help us look
to you, offering your healing touch in a broken world. Amen.*

SECOND SUNDAY

in Lent

Today is Sunday. Push pause. Tune in.

Pay attention to what you're paying attention to today.

What do you notice?

What do you see?
What do you smell?
What do you hear?
What do you taste?
What do you feel?

Use the following page to capture or respond to what you are noticing.

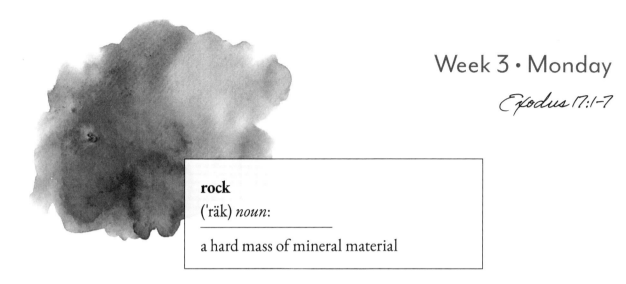

Exodus 17:1-7

> **rock**
>
> ('räk) *noun*:
> _____
>
> a hard mass of mineral material

The LORD said to Moses . . . "Hit the rock. Water will
come out of it, and the people will be able to drink."

—Exodus 17:5, 6

The Israelites face a real and present fear over their very survival. Their basic human needs can't be met in this desert wilderness. In his frustration, Moses cries out to the Lord, fearful for his own life, "[These people] are getting ready to stone me" (v. 4). But instead of being used as a weapon, the rock becomes a source of the Lord's salvation. In this wilderness, the Israelites are not alone. God is with them, and God will provide what they need.

The Lenten journey takes us through the wilderness. We are confronted with wilderness stories of scarcity, wandering, and fear. In these stories, we are reminded that in our very human experiences, God meets us again and again. When we cry out, God is there, providing what we need.

For what are you crying out to God?

Come to our aid, O Lord. We are weary in the wilderness of our world.
You are our rock. Pour out your salvation on us. Amen.

water

(wó:tər) *noun*:

a colorless, odorless compound composed
of hydrogen and oxygen

All of you who are thirsty, come to the water!
—Isaiah 55:1

The prophet Isaiah writes to a community adrift and in conflict. He shares a message from God: repent and return to being a community grounded in faithfulness and receive abundant life for all. For those who are thirsty, there will be water to drink; for those who are hungry, there will be food to eat.

We know what it feels like to be adrift, don't we? We certainly know what it feels like to be in conflict. It's a part of our universal human experience. These verses from Isaiah can feel personal. We feel isolated, alone, under attack, ashamed, thirsty. Isaiah's call to repentance and community echoes throughout time. Let us return to the Lord with repentant hearts. The Lord's living waters are there to nourish us all.

Where in your life are you thirsty? How are you being called to experience God's abundance?

*We confess, O Lord, that we are thirsty. Your living water is abundant. Help
us to open ourselves to receive your generous forgiveness. Amen.*

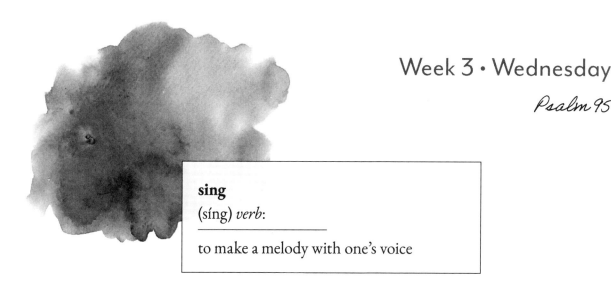

sing

(síng) *verb*:

_____

to make a melody with one's voice

Come, let's sing out loud to the Lᴏʀᴅ!
Let's raise a joyful shout to the rock of our salvation!
—Psalm 95:1

The psalms cover the spectrum of the human experience: from lament and sorrow to overflowing shouts of joy, it's all there. Whether in joy or in suffering, the psalms always praise God. Psalm 95 communicates clearly why we praise God: God reigns. In a world that resists God's way of love, Psalm 95 calls us back to praise the God who reigns over all.

The folk hymn "My Life Flows On" echoes the psalmist's posture of praise despite all that the world can throw at us. "Through all the tumult and the strife, I hear the music ringing. It finds an echo in my soul. How can I keep from singing?" We walk the Lenten journey acknowledging the complexity of our humanity. And, by God's grace, "through all the tumult and the strife," we sing out to the Lord. How might you sing out to God today?

*Lord of heaven and earth, even in our wilderness wandering, we turn to you with songs
and shouts of praise. Keep our hearts open to follow where you lead. Amen.*

sheep

(ˈshēp) *noun*:

a livestock animal often raised for wool
or meat

Come, let's worship and bow down!
    Let's kneel before the LORD, our maker!
He is our God,
    and we are the people of his pasture,
    the sheep in his hands.

    —Psalm 95:6-7

In both the Old and New Testament, God is portrayed as a caring shepherd watching over sheep. In the ancient world, honorable kings were often portrayed as good shepherds who were steadfast in caring for their sheep. The connection of God as shepherd and God as the one who reigns over all and is deserving of worship is at the heart of Psalm 95.

Sheep wander and need diligent care from their caregivers. God's children, too, are prone to wander from God's way of love. The season of Lent provides us with time to be mindful of our waywardness and to return to faithfully pursue the God of all that is.

How do you relate to the idea of being a sheep in God's pasture, held in God's hand?

*God, you are the Good Shepherd. You watch over and care for us, even when we wander
away from you. Help us to return to you with hearts of praise and adoration. Amen.*

Romans 5:1–11

> pour
>
> (pór) *verb*:
> _____
>
> to move a liquid or fluid from one
> container to another; to flow or fall

The love of God has been poured out in our hearts through the Holy Spirit, who has been given to us.

—Romans 5:5

The apostle Paul writes to a persecuted community, one confronted with real threats. Hope is hard to find in a world like theirs. Paul encourages them to remember the source of their hope: God's love. God's is a limitless, extravagant love that can keep us going even in the most unimaginable circumstances.

We began the Lenten season by confronting the reality of our mortality: *from dust you came and to dust you shall return*. The journey of the Lenten season takes us to the death of our God on a cross. Where is hope in such a season? Paul reminds us that even when things are impossibly difficult, by the grace of God's love poured into us, we have hope.

Where have you experienced God's love poured out?

You have poured your love into us, O God. Such extravagant love
sustains us in all things. Thank you, God. Thank you.

drink

(driŋk) *verb*:

to take a liquid beverage into the mouth and swallow

Whoever drinks from the water that I will give will never be thirsty again. The water that I give will become in those who drink it a spring of water that bubbles up into eternal life.

—John 4:14

Who gets a drink? Who gets a seat at the table? Who gets an invitation? Jesus' visit to a well becomes an opportunity for the Samaritan woman, a person living on the margins, to receive so much more than a drink of water. Jesus makes it clear that in God's world, she gets a drink, an invitation, and a seat at the table.

It is a very human characteristic to draw lines and differentiate between "us" and "them." This perspective, though, leads to a scarcity mindset. We easily start to believe that resources are finite and we must grab them for "us" and "our people." In the interaction between Jesus and the Samaritan woman, Jesus makes it clear that God's all-inclusive, sustaining love is poured out and flows as living water that is available to all. There is no limit to God's love.

Where have you observed God's living water bubbling up?

God, open our hearts to see where your living water is bubbling up around us. Give us the strength and wisdom to be partners in breaking down barriers so that all may experience your love poured out. Amen.

THIRD SUNDAY
in Lent

Today is Sunday. Push pause. Tune in.

Pay attention to what you're paying attention to today.

What do you notice?

What do you see?
What do you smell?
What do you hear?
What do you taste?
What do you feel?

Use the following page to capture or respond to what you are noticing.

heart

('härt) *noun*:

the emotional center or total of a person's character or personality

The LORD said to Samuel, "Have no regard for his appearance or stature, because I haven't selected him. God doesn't look at things like humans do. Humans see only what is visible to the eyes, but the LORD sees into the heart."

—1 Samuel 16:7

Saul is a failed king. God has made that clear. Despite his grief, Samuel has a priestly duty to anoint the next king of Israel. When Samuel is introduced to Jesse's oldest son, the handsome Eliab, Samuel believes this is the one he was sent to anoint. Immediately, the Lord rebukes Samuel. God sees differently than Samuel. Ultimately, God's choice is based on character and heart, not on stature.

Decision-making is a necessary part of each person's journey of faith. In this text from 1 Samuel, we are reminded that we must attune our hearts to God's heart when discerning a faithful path. God's ways are not our ways. If we are to practice faithfulness throughout our lives, we must be mindful that God sees the world differently than we do. To align oneself with God's heart, a person must pursue a life of character and integrity.

What do you imagine is at the center of God's heart?

God of love, make our ways your ways that we may live as faithful followers in the world. Amen.

shepherd

(shep-ərd) *noun*:

_____

a person who tends to and protects sheep

The LORD is my shepherd.
I lack nothing.

—Psalm 23:1

Psalm 23 is perhaps the most well-known chapter in the entire Bible. In pop culture, it is often seen as a simple piece of poetry to convey tranquility or a song recited at funerals to deliver comfort. While we can find a peaceful comfort in Psalm 23, this psalm is more so a song of praise about the steadfastness of God. God is the provider of everything we need: food, shelter, protection. The Lord, our Good Shepherd, provides.

Our world, especially in Western culture, is propped up by a scarcity mindset. We are inundated with advertisements for what we need and messages about how our lives are incomplete without a long list of luxuries. Psalm 23 stands in stark opposition to these messages. What do we need to make it in this rough-and-tumble world? The Lord.

How does the image of God as a shepherd resonate with you?

You are the Good Shepherd. With you, we lack nothing. Thank you, Lord! Amen.

> **house**
>
> ('haủs) *noun*:
> _____
>
> a structure where people live; a dwelling

> Yes, goodness and faithful love
>   will pursue me all the days of my life,
>   and I will live in the LORD's house
>   as long as I live.
>
> —Psalm 23:6

We belong to God. Period. This promise is at the heart of Psalm 23. God's love, protection, and care are always pursuing us. This promise is deeply personal and expansive. God's abiding love is for each of us and extends to the world. God's household includes "every part of the earth" (Ps 22:27).

In the season of Lent, we are confronted by our own brokenness and mortality. Psalm 23 offers us an oasis in our desert wandering. Even in our weariness, the house of the Lord remains forever, offering protection and care.

What do you imagine the Lord's house looks like?

You, O God, are a gracious host. In our wonder, we look to you, knowing that your steadfast love is always with us. Thank you, God! Amen.

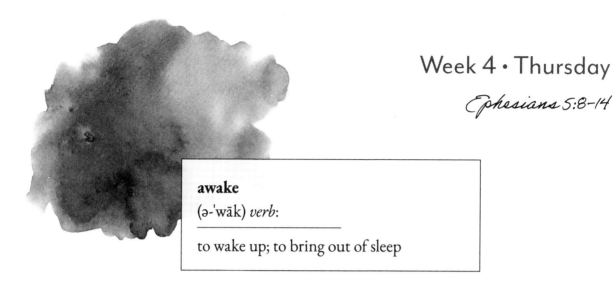

awake

(ə-ˈwāk) *verb*:

_____

to wake up; to bring out of sleep

Wake up, sleeper! Get up from the dead, and
Christ will shine on you.

—Ephesians 5:14

Christianity is a holistic faith. To walk in the way of Christ is a matter of the mind, heart, hands, and feet. While learning about what it is to follow Christ, it's important to remember that our actions matter. These verses from Ephesians remind us to be diligent followers of Christ, staying awake to God's work in and through us.

The ebb and flow of the church calendar offers us special windows of time that remind us to stay alert, to pay attention. Lent is one such season. Be curious today about what you're paying attention to on your faith journey.

How has your Lenten practice impacted your Lenten journey? What are you awake to?

*Shine your light on me! Awaken me to your work in the world, that
I may follow you faithfully all the days of my life. Amen.*

world

(ˈwər(-ə)ld) *noun*:

the earth or globe; a dwelling place for humans

God so loved the world that he gave his only Son, so that everyone who believes in him won't perish but will have eternal life. God didn't send his Son into the world to judge the world, but that the world might be saved through him.

—John 3:16-17

John 3 presents us with a challenge. Because these verses are so widely used in both secular and religious spaces, we often carry our own interpretation to the text. But Jesus' monologue here insists that we set aside what we know and open ourselves to being changed by God through Jesus.

Read through this text with a spirit of curiosity. Do you notice something you haven't before? Consider how these statements challenge your faith: God is with us. God loves us. And the "us" is the whole world.

What does a world shaped by God's love look like?

God, your love is more than we can know. Open us up to be changed by your love, that the world may know your mercy and grace through us. Amen.

> **celebrate**
>
> ('se-lə-ˌbrāt) *verb*:
> _____
>
> to observe a holiday or event with
> festivities or ceremonies

"This son of mine was dead and has come back to life! He was lost and is found!" And they began to celebrate.

—Luke 15:24

This text is one of Christianity's most beloved parables. The images of a father, sons, and complicated relationships immediately draw in the reader. Sitting with the complications invites us to take an interpretive approach. Is it a story about a repentant son, a forgiving father, or a wronged brother who was mistreated? It's a story with so many layers. But at the center is celebration.

Lent is a season of repentance, of coming face to face with our mortality. It is often a somber time, when our prayers and our hymns trudge along to indicate our penitence. Is there a place for celebration in Lent? Yes, there is. Our world is filled with sharp edges and grief. Despair always lurks. What if the invitation to celebrate in this text isn't just for the father's household? It extends to us, too. Celebration is an alternative to despair. The father is quick to celebrate. We can be, as well.

What are you being invited to celebrate?

Turn our tears into dancing, O Lord. Open our hearts to celebrate your work all around us. Amen.

FOURTH SUNDAY
in Lent

Today is Sunday. Push pause. Tune in.

Pay attention to what you're paying attention to today.

What do you notice?

What do you see?
What do you smell?
What do you hear?
What do you taste?
What do you feel?

Use the following page to capture or respond to what you are noticing.

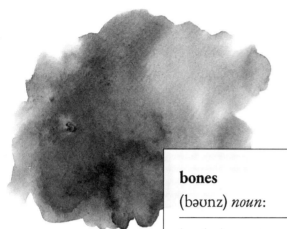

bones

(bəʊnz) *noun*:

hard, dense tissue that, when put
together, forms a skeleton

[The Lord] said to me, "Prophesy over these bones, and say to them, Dry
bones, hear the Lord's word! The Lord God proclaims to these bones: I
am about to put breath in you, and you will live again."

—Ezekiel 37:4-5

The images of these verses from the prophet Ezekiel are rich and pointed. Ezekiel has been writing
to a community in despair. They are completely hopeless. Ezekiel sees their hopelessness as a val-
ley of bones—a stark image of overwhelming death—and they were "very dry." "Can the bones live
again?" the Lord asks.

Understandably, Western cultures exist on the edge of despair and hopelessness. Social isolation,
environmental issues, and widespread discrimination are just a tip of the iceberg of what is contribut-
ing to what professionals are calling a mental health crisis in the United States. We don't have to stretch
our imaginations to ask the existential question with EzekielL "Will we survive this?" Let these words
settle into your bones, "I am about to put breath in you, and you will live again." Yes, beloved, you will.
God is with you. "This is what the Lord says."

Where do you see very dry bones and wonder, "Can these bones live?"

*God, you are always with us. When we find ourselves falling into hopelessness and despair, you
ask us, "Can these bones live?" Give us the faith to respond, "Lord God, only you know." Amen.*

engrave

(in-ˈgrāv) *verb*:

to inscribe or print permanently on a surface

I will put my Instructions within them and engrave them on their hearts. I will be their God, and they will be my people.

—Jeremiah 31:33b

These verses are central to a Judeo-Christian understanding of God's covenant. God's covenant is an integral part of a person's identity. It is interwoven into the whole self. God's covenant written on stone, tablet, or even in a holy book is not enough: it must also be a part of a person's life blood.

This idea of God's covenant engraved on one's heart offers both a challenge and a promise. In many ways, the season of Lent reminds us that we are at a crossroads, similar to what we read in Jeremiah. Our faith is not something that we can simply take on and take off. The challenge is for our faith to be fully integrated into our lives. Our Lenten journey opens a path of faithfulness that invites our whole self to be present to and with God. God's promises and love are written on our heart. We belong to God.

How does your understanding of this text affect how you live in the world?

You have engraved your promises on my heart, O God. May my life reflect your promises of hope and love in the world. Amen.

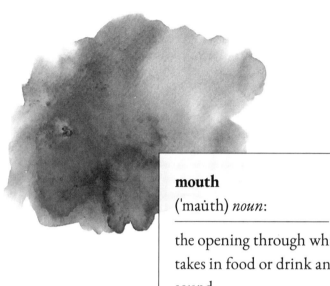

> **mouth**
>
> (ˈmau̇th) *noun*:
> _____
>
> the opening through which an animal
> takes in food or drink and vocalizes
> sound

When the LORD changed Zion's circumstances for the better,
  it was like we had been dreaming.
Our mouths were suddenly filled with laughter;
  our tongues were filled with joyful shouts.

—Psalm 126:1-2a

The psalmist depends on the use of memory in unsettled times. Looking back, the psalmist remembers when God delivered God's people. God's people came together in praise and thanksgiving with laughter and shouts of joy.

We are often quick to discard the past, choosing instead to look forward. But the psalmist reminds us that when we remember where we've been, we see signs of where God has delivered us in times of despair. When we see God's salvation at work, we are moved to worship. Our mouths are filled with praise!

When was a time that the Lord changed your circumstances for the better, filling your mouth with joyful shouts?

*God, we remember your acts of deliverance and salvation and we are moved
to praise. Open our mouths in praise for your mighty acts! Amen.*

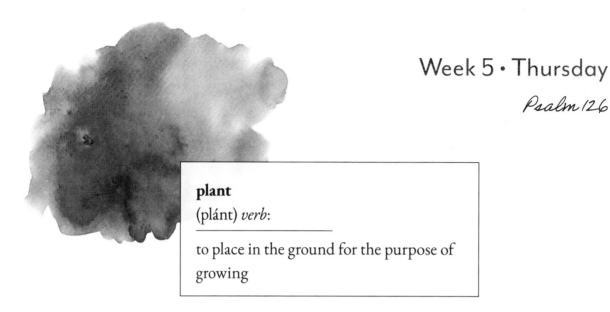

plant

(plánt) *verb*:

_____

to place in the ground for the purpose of growing

Let those who plant with tears
    reap the harvest with joyful shouts.
                      —Psalm 126:5

In the second half of Psalm 126, the psalmist turns from remembering God's acts of salvation to looking ahead with hopeful anticipation. The despair of yesterday becomes the seeds that grow into the promise of tomorrow. The psalmist remembers how God has saved God's people before. Now they are calling on God to "change our circumstances for the better," again.

This psalm gets to the heart of our Lenten journey. Our understanding of God's salvation at work in Jesus Christ puts us in the shoes of the psalmist. In Lent, we stand in the shadow of death, knowing that persecution and, ultimately, crucifixion are central parts of the story. We also know that resurrection is on the other side of crucifixion. We look forward, knowing that God will indeed turn our tears into joyful shouts.

What seeds might your tears be planting?

"Lord, change our circumstances for the better . . . Let those who go out, crying and carrying their seed, come home with joyful shouts, carrying bales of grain!" Amen.

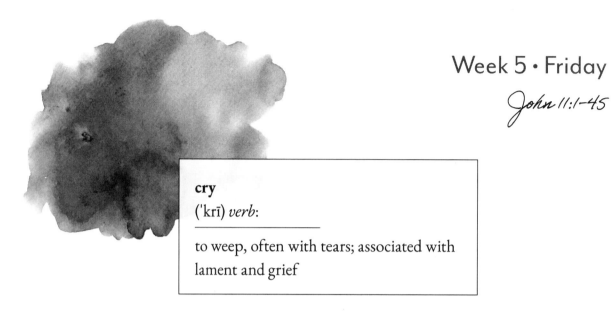

cry

('krī) *verb*:

to weep, often with tears; associated with lament and grief

When Jesus saw [Mary] crying and the Jews who had come with her crying also, he was deeply disturbed and troubled. He asked, "Where have you laid him?" They replied, "Lord, come and see." Jesus began to cry. The Jews said, "See how much he loved him!"

—John 11:33-36

These verses are filled with strong emotions from Jesus. Various translations make interpretive decisions. The NRSV and NIV translations interpret that Jesus is "deeply moved," "greatly disturbed," and "troubled." A more direct translation from the Greek text would be that Jesus is indignant and agitated. Jesus is angry. It's difficult to understand exactly why Jesus is angry, but the Greek makes it clear that Jesus' tears shouldn't be understood as gentle and mild. Lazarus's death isn't a soft loss for Jesus. It is a deep death blow.

Grief carries with it a unique process and journey for each person and each loss. Death carries strong feelings of sadness, anger, and a whole host of other emotions. In this narrative, we see Jesus indignant in the face of death, moved to tears of anger over a deep loss. We should not try to gloss over the sting of death that Jesus feels here, or that we experience in our own lives.

When do you think God might cry tears of indignation?

God, you weep for a world and people experiencing the sting of death. We cry with you. Make haste for your world where tears are turned into joy. Amen.

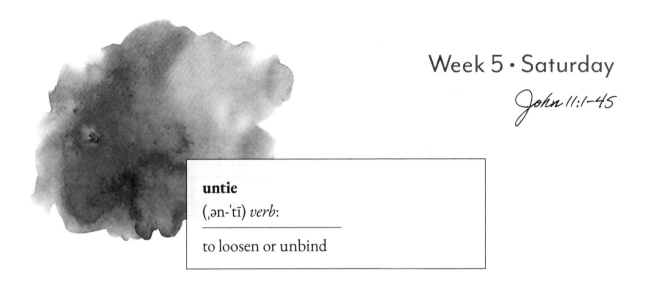

untie

(ˌən-ˈtī) *verb*:

to loosen or unbind

Jesus shouted with a loud voice, "Lazarus, come out!" The dead man came out, his feet bound and his hands tied, and his face covered with a cloth. Jesus said to them, "Untie him and let him go."

—John 11:43-44

As we draw nearer to Holy Week, the cross, and the grave, the stories foretelling Jesus' death become more pointed. The story of Lazarus's resurrection has many direct parallels to Jesus' own resurrection. This story gives the reader a preview of what is to come. When Jesus commands Lazarus to come out of the grave, it is by Jesus' own words that life is fully restored. Lazarus was still in his grave clothes, and it is by Jesus' own words, "Untie him," that Lazarus leaves death behind. Jesus' life-giving work was undeniable.

Jesus' work is to restore life to a world wrapped in grave clothes. Jesus' question to Martha is at the heart of Christian faithfulness. "Do you believe this?" Jesus asks us. With Martha we respond, "Yes, Lord." With that assurance, we go into the world with hopeful expectation that Jesus is calling forth life all around us.

When have you witnessed Jesus' life-giving work?

You, O Lord, are the resurrection and the life. Untie us and let us go into
your world bearing witness to your life-giving work. Amen.

FIFTH SUNDAY
in Lent

Today is Sunday. Push pause. Tune in.

Pay attention to what you're paying attention to today.

What do you notice?

What do you see?
What do you smell?
What do you hear?
What do you taste?
What do you feel?

Use the following page to capture or respond to what you are noticing.

gate

('gāt) *noun*:

a hinged opening in a structure permitting passage

Open the gates of righteousness for me
   so that I can come in and give thanks to the LORD!
This is the LORD's gate;
   those who are righteous enter through it.

—Psalm 118:19-20

In the Revised Common Lectionary (a three-year cycle of scriptures to be used for worship and study), Psalm 118 bookends the liturgy for Palm Sunday and Easter Sunday for all three years. This psalm therefore serves as a hymn for both Jesus' entry into Jerusalem leading to his crucifixion and death and then for his resurrection. Many moments happen between Palm Sunday and Easter Sunday, but this psalm is placed at both the beginning and end as a reminder that, at every moment, God's faithfulness always calls us to exuberant praise and thanksgiving.

As we draw closer to Holy Week, the climax of our Lenten journey, we prepare ourselves to humbly walk the Jerusalem road with Jesus. With praise and thanksgiving, we enter the Lord's gates. We know that God's righteous mercy and grace go before us. We enter with thanks to the Lord!

What do you imagine the Lord's gates of mercy and grace hold for you in this season?

*We enter your gates with thanksgiving, O Lord. Prepare our hearts
to walk the Jerusalem journey with you. Amen.*

foundation stone

(faùn-ˈdā-shən + ˈstōn) *noun*:

a cornerstone; a point at which two masonry walls come together at a structure's base

I thank you because you answered me,
     because you were my saving help.
The stone rejected by the builders
     is now the main foundation stone!

—Psalm 118:21-22

Take a moment to imagine a construction site filled with stones. When it comes time to choose the stone that will provide the foundation for the entire building, the builders begin by discarding those stones that they think won't work. The pile of rejected stones is where the Lord's work begins. It is from what was considered rubble that God chose the foundation of the work. What a surprise!

God's work of salvation is full of surprises. What is foolish to the world is often where God's work of salvation begins. As we come closer to Holy Week, we can get curious about the places in our lives that we would like to hide or discard. How might God be at work in those rejected places?

How is God's foundation stone supporting you in this season?

We thank you, O Lord, because you answer us and are our saving help.
Open our hearts to your work in the rejected places of our lives and the
world that we might participate in your acts of salvation. Amen.

task

('task) *noun*:

---

assigned work that needs to be completed within a set time frame

When they approached Jerusalem and came to Bethpage on the Mount of Olives, Jesus gave two disciples a task.
He said to them, "Go into the village over there. As soon as you enter, you will find a donkey tied up and a colt with it. Untie them and bring them to me."

—Matthew 21:1-2

As Jesus prepares to enter Jerusalem, we know that the climax of the Lenten journey is closing in on us. Rather than speeding up, though, the story seems to slow down in these opening verses of Matthew 21. Jesus doesn't tear into the city as a victorious king might. The text is paced, deliberate, and detailed. Jesus gives the disciples a task, and they follow through. As he prepares for this final journey, Jesus' authority is humble and steadfast.

There is a temptation to rush from Palm Sunday to Easter Sunday. Perhaps we can take a cue from Matthew's Gospel and slow down. Take in the details of the story. Notice which parts stand out.

How might you slow down and give yourself space to experience Holy Week?

Blessed is the one who comes in the name of the Lord! Slow us down and open our hearts that we may discover anew what it is to follow you. Amen.

Matthew 21:1–11

king

('kiŋ) *noun*:

_____

a ruler or monarch; the official head of an independent state

Now this happened to fulfill what the prophet said, *say to Daughter Zion, "Look, your king is coming to you, humble and riding on a donkey, and on a colt the donkey's offspring."*

—Matthew 21:4-5

The gospel writers wanted to make it very clear that Jesus was indeed the Messiah, the anointed one whom God sent into the world. It's in our human nature to look for a ruler or leader. Jesus is the one we're looking for. The question is always there, though, of what kind of a ruler or leader is Jesus. These verses provide the most foundational clarity about what kind of king Jesus is. He is the one we've been looking for, the anointed. He is humble and brings peace.

"King" is a title that comes with a lot of complicated views. For many, it elicits a masculine image of rule by violence and oppression. This text challenges this by claiming that Jesus is king and that his rule is defined by humility, peace, and life.

What does "Jesus is king" mean to you? What other titles for Jesus are meaningful to you?

God, you rule with humility and peace. May we faithfully follow you, walking in your path of peace. Amen.

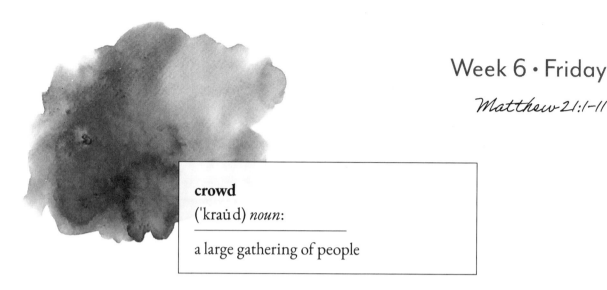

crowd

(ˈkrau̇d) *noun*:

_____

a large gathering of people

The crowds in front of him and behind him shouted, *"Hosanna* to the Son of David! *Blessings on the one who comes in the name of the Lord! Hosanna* in the highest!"

—Matthew 21:9

The original hearers of this text would have connected the crowds lining the streets for Jesus' entry into Jerusalem with a king or ruler's triumphant entry after a battle. Matthew certainly wants to communicate that Jesus is the ruler, but the irony is that Jesus' battle is just beginning. Even more, the ending, at first, will not look like a victory but crucifixion. There is a crowd gathered to bear witness to Jesus' entry, but they will not stay the course for what lies ahead.

Palm Sunday and Easter Sunday have historically been two Sundays of the year that churches expect larger crowds. People show up to shout "Hosanna!" and again a week later to cheer, "Christ is risen!" But there is a lot of somber silence in between. The crowd quickly grows thin. We are invited to stay the course, to continue following Jesus, the humble ruler.

What would a gathered crowd welcoming Jesus, the humble ruler, look like today? Are we who follow Jesus today any more prepared for the silence that is to come?

God, we come together with shouts of praise for you. Give us strength and courage for the days ahead to stay the course of peace and humility. Amen.

palm

('pälm) *noun*:

a branchless tree or bush with long ridged
leaves

Now a large crowd spread their clothes on the road. Others cut palm
branches off the trees and spread them on the road.

—Matthew 21:8

The cloaks and palm branches laid out on the ground for Jesus' entry into Jerusalem are another way
in which Matthew clearly portrays Jesus as the Messiah, the one whom God's people have been
waiting for. For Greco-Romans, palm leaves were a symbol of victory. The gathered crowd would have
understood the context. They were, indeed, welcoming their victorious leader.

Matthew 21:1-11 is filled with vivid images of Jesus' entry into Jerusalem. Christians have re-
membered this story for centuries by waving palms and gathering in crowds to march around city
blocks and churches. As we prepare to enter Holy Week, reflect on how the story of Jesus' entry into
Jerusalem speaks to you this year. How do you experience the power of the text? What questions do
you carry with you?

Where does your hope in Jesus as victorious leader lie?

We welcome you, O Lord. We open our palms in praise to you, our victorious God. Amen.

SIXTH SUNDAY

in Lent

Palm/Passion Sunday

Today is Sunday. Push pause. Tune in.

Pay attention to what you're paying attention to today.

What do you notice?

What do you see?
What do you smell?
What do you hear?
What do you taste?
What do you feel?

Use the following page to capture or respond to what you are noticing.

> **perfume**
>
> (ˈpər-ˌfyüm) *noun*:
> _____
>
> a substance often made of oils and natural fragrances with a pleasant scent

Then Mary took an extraordinary amount, almost three-quarters of a pound, of very expensive perfume made of pure nard. She anointed Jesus' feet with it, then wiped his feet dry with her hair. The house was filled with the aroma of the perfume.

—John 12:3

As we enter Holy Week, the tone of this text is foreboding. Mary performs an act on Jesus associated with preparing a body for burial. Even with death looming, Mary's act of discipleship and expression of extravagant love takes center stage. With a grandiose gesture, she uses an "extraordinary amount . . . of very expensive perfume" to anoint Jesus' feet. The house is filled not with the smell of death, but of love poured out.

At this point in John's Gospel, we sense a shift. The crucifixion and death of Jesus are imminent. The weight of anticipated grief is heavy. But this story serves as a powerful reminder that God's all-encompassing love surrounds us—even in such a time as this.

How do you experience God's love surrounding you, like a house filled with the aroma of perfume poured out?

God, open our hearts to be like Mary, pouring ourselves out in love for you and the world. Amen.

Holy Week • Tuesday

John 12:20-36

clock

('kläk) *noun*:

_____

an instrument for measuring time

Jesus replied, "The time has come for the Human One to be glorified."

—John 12:23

This spot in Jesus' Jerusalem journey marks a point of no return. Jesus had set his eyes toward Jerusalem. He then entered Jerusalem. He has now set his feet in the direction of the cross. We might apply the modern phrase to Jesus' words, "The clock is ticking." Even in such an ominous text, God continues to reach out with reassurance: "A voice came from heaven, 'I have glorified it, and I will glorify it again'" (v. 28).

The Holy Week texts are the same year after year. While the words might repeat, what we carry with us changes. The story remains the same; we who encounter the story are changed from year to year.

What is shifting in you? How might God be reassuring you at this time?

God, you are glorified. We look to you with unsettled spirits, knowing that you are at work to glorify what has been, what is, and what will be. Thank you, God. Amen.

Holy Week • Wednesday

John 13:21-32

> **night**
>
> (ˈnīt) *noun*:
> _____
>
> the period between sunset and sunrise
> when there is darkness

So when Judas took the bread, he left immediately.
And it was night.

—John 13:30

Some Christian traditions refer to the Wednesday of Holy Week as "Spy Wednesday." The text for this day reveals Judas's plans to betray Jesus. Judas's position in the narrative represents the intersection of many contrasts: day and night, obedience and betrayal, and, ultimately, life and death. Judas is the one who betrays Jesus, exits into the night, and, ultimately, chooses death over life.

Judas has a place at the table. Jesus offers him hospitality and bread, a symbol for life. He is invited into obedience and the life found in Jesus. But heartbreakingly, Judas chooses to walk away and into the night. While very few choices we face are so straightforward, we are still regularly faced with decisions. We can consider where God is extending an invitation to obedience and life in our own lives and where we find ourselves resisting.

Where do you see yourself in this story? How do you experience the contrast between day and night?

In Jesus Christ, you are glorified, O God. Give us the wisdom and
courage to step into your light, living obediently to you. Amen.

Holy Week • Maundy Thursday

John 13:1–17, 31b–35

> **basin**
>
> (ˈbā-sᵊn) *noun*:
> _____
>
> a vessel or bowl used to hold water for
> rinsing or washing

[Jesus] got up from the table and took off his robes. Picking up a linen towel, he tied it around his waist. Then he poured water into a washbasin and began to wash the disciples' feet, drying them with the towel he was wearing.

—John 13:4-5

Many Christian communities around the world practice foot washing on Maundy Thursday, the Thursday of Holy Week. For many modern worshipers, this is an awkward practice. But it's always been awkward. Peter normalized the strangeness for us. "Lord, are you going to wash my feet?" he asked. Jesus' act of washing the disciples' feet exemplifies Jesus as both Lord and servant. Both are central to his identity, and as Jesus' followers, one way we follow Jesus is as servants to all.

The end of the day on Maundy Thursday marks the beginning of three of Christianity's most holy days. Tradition refers to these three days as the Holy Triduum. These three sacred days begin with this narrative of the Lord Jesus identifying himself as servant to all.

Take some time to reflect on the strangeness of Jesus as Lord and Servant. How are you being served? How are you being called to serve? How does each of these roles feel?

Lord, fill us with your humility and courage to serve one another as you showed us. Amen.

Holy Week • Good Friday

John 18:1–19:37

---

cross

('kros) *noun*:

a structure consisting of a horizontal and vertical piece; an ancient form of execution

---

Carrying his cross by himself, he went out to a place called Skull Place (in Aramaic, *Golgotha*). That's where they crucified him—and two others with him, one on each side and Jesus in the middle.

—John 19:17-18

The cross is the culmination of our Lenten journey. Whenever we experience isolation and despair, the cross is always present as a reminder that God knows the depths of our sorrow and grief. "Were you there when they crucified my Lord?" the old spiritual asks. Yes, God was there. Yes, God is with you.

It is tempting to rush grief. Our Western culture generally takes a "let's get on with it" approach to suffering. As painful as it is, the story of Jesus' crucifixion and murder reflects a God who is with us, not abandoning or denying the bitterness of being human. We join Mary in the shadow of the cross and sing the old song, "Sometimes it causes me to tremble."

How are you experiencing the shadow of the cross?

O God, on the cross, you knew the depth of human suffering. We come to you with prayers for those for whom isolation, grief, and despair are no stranger. Give us your mercy, God. Amen.

John 19:38-42

> **tomb**
>
> ('tüm) *noun*:
> _____
>
> a place set aside for burying human remains; a grave

There was a garden in the place where Jesus was crucified, and in the garden was a new tomb in which no one had ever been laid. Because it was the Jewish Preparation Day and the tomb was nearby, they laid Jesus in it.

—John 19:41-42

Holy Saturday is a day for settling into liminal space. We stand between the despair of Good Friday and the exuberant joy of Easter Sunday. We're no longer "there," but we haven't yet arrived "there" either. Sanctuaries remain empty or covered in the black cloths of Good Friday services, but the people have scattered and leave the spaces empty. Much like a tomb, the silence of the day is sharp.

On this Holy Saturday, we can give ourselves permission to settle into silence. We may still be experiencing the chaotic despair of Good Friday. Or we might already be anticipating the mystery of Easter. Wherever we find ourselves, we can embrace the power of sitting in the moment, considering the wonder of the "now and not yet" of Holy Saturday.

How do you experience the wonder of the tomb?

Gracious God, we come to you in the silence of the tomb. We grieve a broken world and find comfort in the mystery of the grave. Amen.

announce

(ə-ˈnaůn(t)s) *verb*:

to make known; to communicate news publicly

Mary Magdalene left and announced to the disciples, "I've seen the Lord." Then she told them what he said to her.

—John 20:18

Alleluia! Christ is Risen! The Lord is Risen indeed!

We arrived at the cross and then the tomb, marking the end of our Lenten journey. While death marks the end of that journey, it is not the end of God's story of salvation. Through expressions of story and creativity, we have experienced together the great mystery of our faith: Christ has died. Christ has risen. Christ will come again. Alleluia!

Mary Magdalene made an announcement: "I have seen the Lord." Through her, we celebrate the Easter promise that Christ is not in the tomb but is alive. Our faith compels us to join that great celebration of saints through the ages. We are to announce that God's story goes on and on as a story of life and love. As Easter people, we too announce the good news that Christ is risen indeed!

How will you announce the good news of the risen Christ this Easter?

God of life, you broke the bonds of death. Alleluia! You have called us to be Easter people, announcing the good news that your life and love never end. Amen.